Focus on India

Natalie Hyde

A Crabtree Forest Book

Crabtree Publishing
crabtreebooks.com

Author: Natalie Hyde

Series research and development: Janine Deschenes

Editorial director: Kathy Middleton

Editor: Ellen Rodger

Proofreader: Melissa Boyce

Design: Tammy McGarr

IMAGE CREDITS

Shutterstock

AbhishekMittal: p. 33 (top); AjayTvm: p. 13 (top right); bodom: p. 10; Cavan-Images: cover (bottom); CherylRamalho: p. 11 (top); CRS PHOTO: p. 44 (bottom), 45 (top); Daniel J. Rao: p. 16 (bottom); Dinesh Hukmani: p. 41 (center); Don Mammoser: p. 14 (bottom); Fred Duval: p. 33 (center); Hari Mahidhar: p. 13 (bottom), 25 (top), 31 (bottom); Ikhwan Ameer: p. 27 (center); ImagesofIndia: p. 19 (top); Im_rohitbhakar: p. 12 (bottom), 14 (center right); Iryna Rasko: p. 8–9 (bottom); Leonid Andronov: p. 15 (bottom); Maneesh Agnihotri: p. 44 (top); Manoej Paateel: p. 26 (bottom), 30 (bottom); Matyas Rehak: p. 17 (center), 23 (top); Michal Knitl: p. 27 (top); Migs Nomad: p. 38 (top); ikadun: p. 26 (top); Mirko Kuzmanovic: p. 18 (bottom left); MOROZ NATALIYA: p. 1; Noppasin Wongchum: p. 42; OmMishra: p. 27 (bottom); Parikh Mahendra N: p. 31 (center), 43 (top); Paulharding00: p. 29 (bottom); PhotographerIncognito: p. 45 (center); PI: p. 35 (center); pjhpix: p. 29 (top); PradeepGaurs: p. 25 (center), p. 30 (top), 37 (bottom), 39 (center), 41 (bottom); Regien Paassen: cover (top right); Radiokafka: p. 12 (top); Rahul Sapra: p. 36 (top); Rajdeep Ray: p. 30 (center); Roop_Dey: p. 45 (bottom);
Rudra Narayan Mitra: p. 4 (bottom); Sanjoy Karmakar: p. 17 (bottom); Santosh Varghese: p. 3 (center left); Shashank Shukla Kotaha: p. 5 (top); Simanta Talukdar: p. 40; Snehal Jeevan Pailkar: p. 32 (bottom), 37 (center); StevenK: p. 32 (top); Subhrajit123: p. 36 (bottom); Sunil prajapati:
p. 23 (center); suprabhat: p. 13 (top left); Talukdar David: p. 5 (bottom); Tingling1: p. 35 (bottom); Travel Stock: p. 24 (bottom right); Ultimate Travel Photos: p. 15 (top); Vivvi Smak: p. 20 (center); Yury Birukov: p. 25 (bottom)

Wikimedia Commons

Adam Jones from Kelowna, BC, Canada: p. 22; collections.vam.ac.uk:item:O16731:painting-portrait-of-east-india-company: p. 21 (bottom); Gary Todd: p. 18 (bottom right) NA: p. 23 (bottom); Photo originale G.DEVRED / Agce ROL: p. 24 (top); www.metmuseum.org:toah:works-of-art:1996.100.1; p. 32 (center); Yann: p. 21 (top left)

All other images from Shutterstock

Crabtree Publishing

crabtreebooks.com **800-387-7650**

In Canada: We acknowledge the financial support of the Government of Canada through the Canada Book Fund for our publishing activities.

Hardcover 978-1-0398-4292-2
Paperback 978-1-0398-4300-4
Ebook (pdf) 978-1-0398-4307-3
Epub 978-1-0398-4313-4

Published in Canada
Crabtree Publishing
616 Welland Avenue
St. Catharines, Ontario
L2M 5V6

Published in the United States
Crabtree Publishing
347 Fifth Avenue
Suite 1402-145
New York, New York, 10016

Library and Archives Canada Cataloguing in Publication
Available at Library and Archives Canada

Library of Congress Cataloging-in-Publication Data
Available at the Library of Congress

Printed in the USA/062024/CG20240201

Contents

Introduction

It is a hot and humid day as farmers head out into their jute fields in Purnea, India. Most have small farms of 10 to 13 acres (4 to 5 hectares) dedicated to this crop **cultivated** in the country's eastern state of Bihar. The grassy plant grows for four months and reaches almost 12 feet (3.7 m) high. Farmers check that the flowers have bloomed but have not set seed. This is the perfect time to harvest. Together with their workers, the farmers use sharp **sickles** to cut the jute plants just above the ground. The plants are then left for two or three days until the leaves fall off. After bundling the stems together, they are taken to a nearby stream to soak in running water for 20 days to help loosen the fibers from the stalk.

Dry jute is sold to jute mills where the fibers are turned into a rough fabric called burlap, used for for cloth, rugs, sacks, and coffee bags. Jute mills are disappearing as synthetic, or human-made, fabrics such as nylon are cheaper to produce.

Jute has been used for making textiles in India for over 5,000 years.

About 55 percent of India's population works the land. Many are small farmers with less than 5 acres (2 hectares) in cultivation.

Each farmer hopes the rains will come and keep the stream high enough and flowing long enough to finish soaking. Only then, after three weeks, will the workers come back to squeeze and hang the bundles to dry on bamboo poles. It is a **labor-intensive** process. Jute has been grown in Purnea for centuries but has recently been on the decline. Farmers can make more money from other crops, and many feel jute farming isn't supported by the government.

Country and Subcontinent

India is the seventh-largest country in the world. It is also the second-most **populated** country, with more than 1 billion people. It shares land borders with Bangladesh, Myanmar, Pakistan, China, Nepal, and Bhutan. Even though it shares borders, it forms a peninsula, which means it is surrounded by ocean on three sides. The southwest coast faces the Arabian Sea and the southeast coast is on the Bay of Bengal. The south is surrounded by the Indian Ocean.

India occupies a large part of South Asia. Together with Bangladesh and most of Pakistan, the three countries form a subcontinent. A subcontinent is a large landmass that is part of a continent. The Indian subcontinent is about 70 million years old. The land that is now India broke away from an early supercontinent called Gondwana. This landmass drifted slowly northward for millions of years until it **collided** with Asia. The movement north pushed up the land where these two landmasses met and created the Himalayan mountain range.

Political Regions

Today India is divided into 28 states and eight **union territories**. While many countries create regions based on geography, India has not. In 1956, the state boundaries were reorganized along cultural and language lines. This means that each state has its own unique history, culture, and festivals.

India also **administers** 1,382 islands. The main island groups are the Andaman and Nicobar Islands in the Bay of Bengal, and Lakshadweep, a group of islands in the Arabian Sea. The Andaman and Nicobar Islands are an extension of the Arakan mountain range. Only the peaks are visible above water. The islands are covered with tropical rain forests. They experience many earthquakes and do not have many inhabitants. The islands of Lakshadweep are coral islands. They have been formed by corals growing on underwater volcanoes. There are no forests on these islands. They also do not rise more than 16 feet (5 m) above sea level. This means they are at risk of being **submerged** with rising sea levels.

The Himalayas create a natural boundary with only a few narrow mountain passes connecting India to the rest of Asia.

Netaji Subhas Chandra Bose Island in the Andaman chain is 0.77 miles (1.25 km) long. It was originally inhabited by **Indigenous** Andamanese peoples.

AT A GLANCE

- **OFFICIAL NAME:** Republic of India
- **NATIONAL CAPITAL:** New Delhi
- **POPULATION:** 1.42 billion
- **OFFICIAL LANGUAGE:** Hindi and English (with 22 recognized main languages)
- **LAND AREA:** 1.269 million square miles (3.287 million sq. km)

CHAPTER 1

The Land

India's landmass can be divided into three distinct areas. The first is the Himalayan mountain range in the north. The **plateau** region in the south is called the Deccan. The area in between the two is called the North Indian Plain.

The Himalayas are known for their several ranges with towering peaks, huge **glaciers**, and deep river gorges which straddle five countries. The Indian portion is known as the Indian Himalayan Region (IHR). The snowfields and glaciers feed the lower valley rivers that cross India. Much of the Himalayan range has poor or rocky soil that is not good for agriculture. However, the soil on the north-facing slopes and foothills is good for growing fruit trees, rice, corn, and millet. Some of the hills in the eastern Himalayas have deep, moist soil, where the famous Darjeeling tea is grown.

The Deccan in the south is a large, flat plateau. On the eastern and western edges of the Deccan are low mountain ranges called the Ghats. The Ghats include the flat coastal plains between the hills and the ocean. The North Indian Plain is also called the Indo-Gangetic Plain. This is because India's largest river, the Ganges, flows through it. Most of the population of India lives in this region. In the east, the area is very dry in winter, but heavy rains cause swampy areas in summer. The North Indian Plain is drier to the west and south, where it becomes the Great Indian, or Thar, Desert.

Goats, sheep, and yaks are herded in the valleys of Jammu and Kashmir.

The Thar Desert includes saltwater lakes such as Sambhar Salt Lake. Hundreds of thousands of tons of clean salt are produced each year.

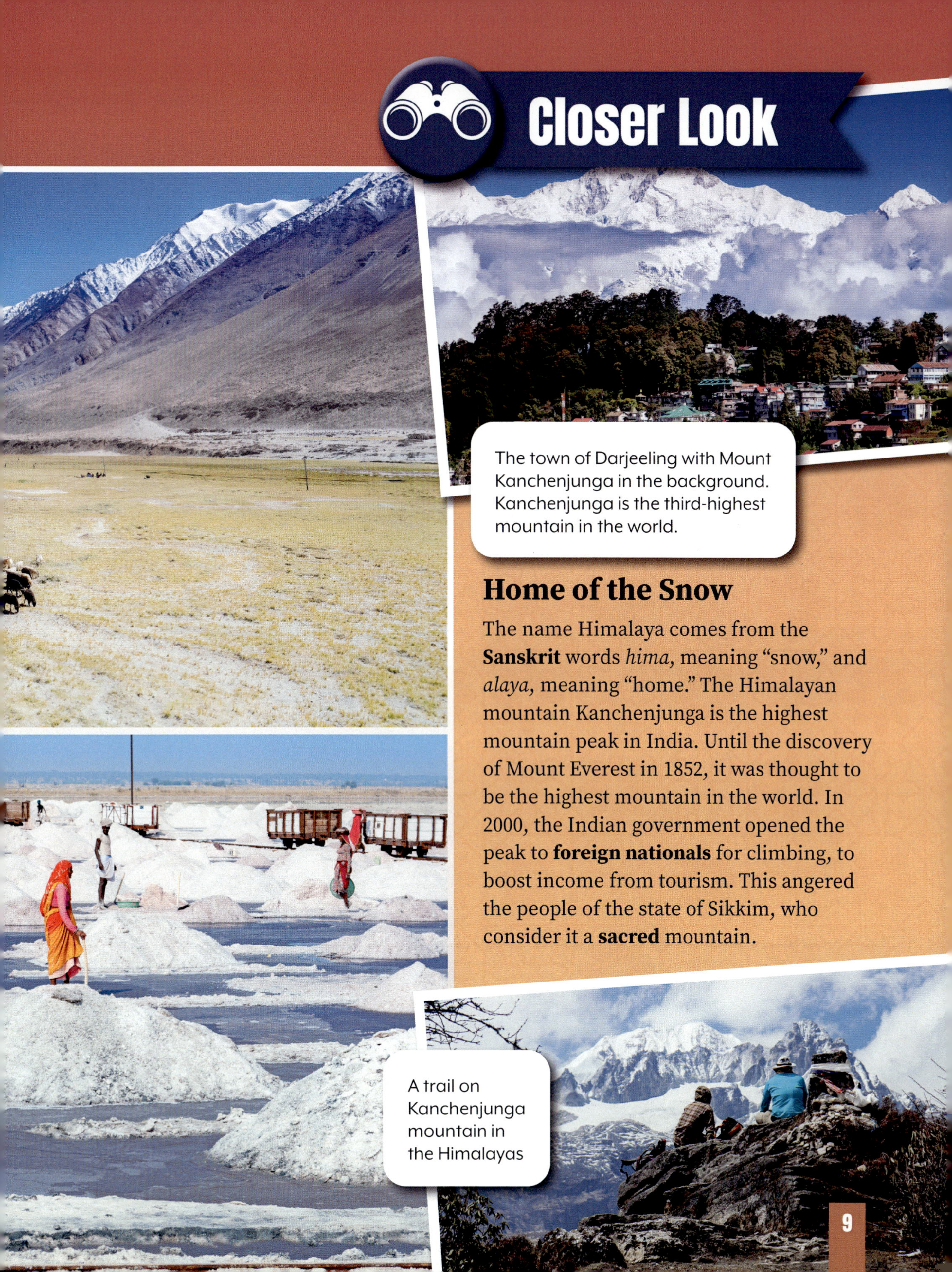

Closer Look

The town of Darjeeling with Mount Kanchenjunga in the background. Kanchenjunga is the third-highest mountain in the world.

Home of the Snow

The name Himalaya comes from the **Sanskrit** words *hima,* meaning "snow," and *alaya,* meaning "home." The Himalayan mountain Kanchenjunga is the highest mountain peak in India. Until the discovery of Mount Everest in 1852, it was thought to be the highest mountain in the world. In 2000, the Indian government opened the peak to **foreign nationals** for climbing, to boost income from tourism. This angered the people of the state of Sikkim, who consider it a **sacred** mountain.

A trail on Kanchenjunga mountain in the Himalayas

The Coast

As India is a peninsula that juts out into the ocean, half of its border is coastline. The coasts are separated from the interior land by the low mountains called Ghats. The western coastal plains are about 31 miles (50 km) wide. The eastern coastal plains are wider, from 62 to 75 miles (100 to 120 km) wide.

The eastern coast, along the Bay of Bengal, is sandy. It has many beaches, lagoons, and offshore sandbars. The eastern coast also has many river deltas. Deltas are wetlands where rivers empty into another body of water such as a lake or ocean. They are formed by the **sediment** carried downstream by the rivers. They create swamp forests and **mangroves**. These areas are home to large crocodiles, pythons, and swamp tigers.

The western coast lies along the Arabian Sea. It is more indented and broken than the eastern coast. Mountain ridges crossing the coastal plain meet the water at some spots. These rocky areas are suitable for shipping ports. The western coast also has many bays, beaches, and flooded valleys called rias.

The Kosi River is called the "Sorrow of Bihar" and is considered India's most destructive river because it often floods.

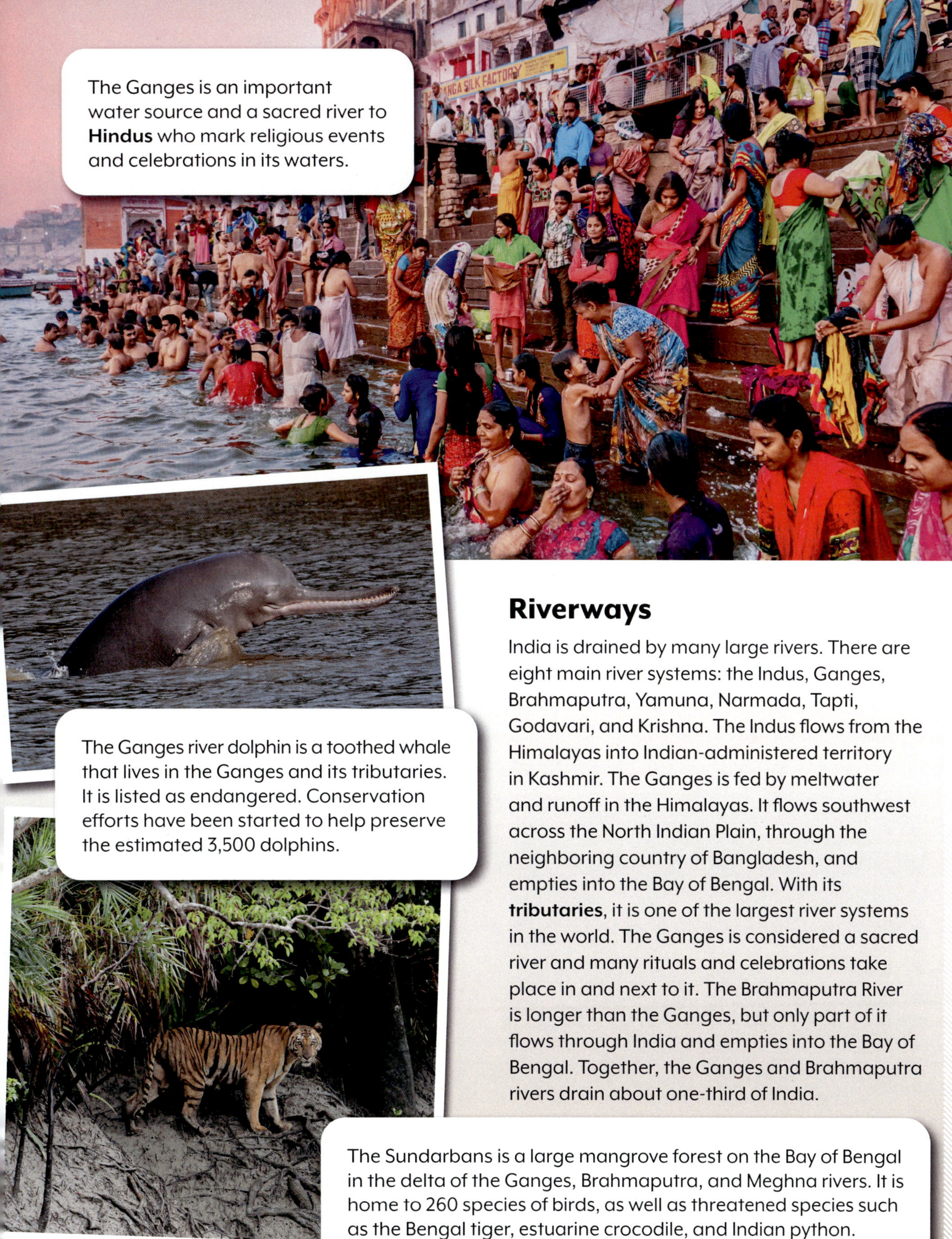

The Ganges is an important water source and a sacred river to **Hindus** who mark religious events and celebrations in its waters.

The Ganges river dolphin is a toothed whale that lives in the Ganges and its tributaries. It is listed as endangered. Conservation efforts have been started to help preserve the estimated 3,500 dolphins.

Riverways

India is drained by many large rivers. There are eight main river systems: the Indus, Ganges, Brahmaputra, Yamuna, Narmada, Tapti, Godavari, and Krishna. The Indus flows from the Himalayas into Indian-administered territory in Kashmir. The Ganges is fed by meltwater and runoff in the Himalayas. It flows southwest across the North Indian Plain, through the neighboring country of Bangladesh, and empties into the Bay of Bengal. With its **tributaries**, it is one of the largest river systems in the world. The Ganges is considered a sacred river and many rituals and celebrations take place in and next to it. The Brahmaputra River is longer than the Ganges, but only part of it flows through India and empties into the Bay of Bengal. Together, the Ganges and Brahmaputra rivers drain about one-third of India.

The Sundarbans is a large mangrove forest on the Bay of Bengal in the delta of the Ganges, Brahmaputra, and Meghna rivers. It is home to 260 species of birds, as well as threatened species such as the Bengal tiger, estuarine crocodile, and Indian python.

Natural Resources

India's landforms, long coastline, and large forests mean the country has many different natural resources such as ores, minerals, forests, farmlands, and fuel sources. This gives India an advantage over other countries that rely on only a few types of resources. If the market or price for one product decreases, India's economy can still do well with other resources.

Incense and incense production are important to India's culture and economy.

The fertile ground means India has a long history of farming, which is important for feeding a large population. Even though a large proportion of Indians eat very little red meat due to religious beliefs, India has the largest cattle population in the world. Livestock is used as draft animals for pulling carts and as meat for non-Hindus. Milk and milk products are an important ingredient in many Indian meals. Livestock also provides leather, and dung is used as fertilizer for crops and as fuel for fires.

A man herds cattle on a road in Rajasthan, a state in northern India. India has more than 27 different breeds of Indigenous cattle.

A lot of sand mining operations in India are illegal because they cause erosion and damage river ecosystems. But in poor regions, this industry is the only way for some families to make money.

Model forests are an attempt to build and protect small forests and natural areas near farms and rivers. In India, model forests help manage storm water for less flooding and better crop irrigation. They also improve air quality.

Mines and Minerals

India has five different mineral belts across the country. As well as metals, it has huge deposits of coal. There are more than 3,000 mines in India, with 550 fuel mines, 560 metal mines, and 1,970 non-metal mines. Fuel mines are petroleum and coal. Non-metal minerals include limestone, ceramic clays, building stones, and diamonds. Five hundred of the metal mines are high-quality iron ore mines. Most of the iron ore is **exported** to China. The rest of these mines are metals such as copper, zinc, lead, gold, and silver.

India is one of the 10 most forest-rich countries in the world. Forestry is an important rural industry. Forest resources include more than just lumber. Indian forests provide latex, gums, resins, essential oils, flavorings, fragrances, incense sticks, and plants used for medicine. India is also the third-largest fish-producing country in the world. Marine resources are not only ocean fish, but also freshwater fish from rivers, canals, ponds, and lakes.

A steel plant in Jharkhand, a state in eastern India that produces 40 percent of the mineral wealth of the country. Jharkhand is also rich in forests.

Population and Settlement

India is one of the most densely populated countries in the world. There are 1,202 people per square mile (464 per sq. km). The population density of the United States is 94 people per sqare mile (36 per sq. km) and Canada has a density of 11 per sqare mile (4 per sq. km). Most people in India live in rural areas. Only 27 percent of people live in cities and towns—yet there are many large cities with populations of 3 to 12 million people.

The North Indian Plain is considered one of the most populated areas in the world. The Ganges River that flows through it brings water for cities, crops, livestock, and transportation. Because the Ganges is considered a sacred river, holy cities have developed along its banks. The least populated areas in India are the Himalayas and the Eastern Ghats, a mountain range in eastern and southern India.

Rice paddies in the Eastern Ghats

For a full year, Indian farmers protested new laws in 2021 that they felt would pay them less for the food they grew by allowing private buyers to set prices and store and hoard food. Roughly 700 people died in violent clashes during the protests. In a rare move, the government backed down on its plan.

A crowded bazaar in New Delhi, India's capital. Bazaars are markets with shops.

Mumbai's Chhatrapati Shivaji International Airport is known for its architecture and art exhibits. The building's columns are styled like peacock feathers. Peacocks are India's national bird.

Rural and City Life

India has historically been an **agrarian society**, with a high proportion of farmers and a large rural population. It produces enough food to feed its population, yet hunger and poor nutrition are still issues. Most farmers are small landholders who have other jobs in addition to farming. **Climate change** has contributed to more **arid** lands and **desertification**, making it even harder for small landholders. Recent Indian agriculture laws attempted to reform and modernize farming by setting up a new marketing system. Farmers complained that the laws were "anti-farmer" and intended to help middlemen buyers and large corporate, or non-family, farms.

Now, more than ever, young people are flocking to cities and towns for jobs and opportunities. But cities are not coping well with the influx. They suffer from shortages of water and affordable homes, transportation, open spaces, and problems with air pollution and traffic. The latest government policies are attempting to improve living standards in towns and cities.

Road and Rail

The road network in India is the second largest in the world, and one of the busiest. India also has the fourth-largest and second-busiest railway network. It moves more than 8 billion passengers and 1.32 billion tons (1.2 billion metric tons) of freight each year. Waterways also help with transport. The rivers, canals, and creeks make it the ninth-largest waterway network in the world. India has hundreds of airports for commercial and cargo flights. Thirty airports serve international travel, while 107 are domestic. There are also smaller airstrips, which are reserved for the military.

Indian Railways is the largest employer in India and one of the largest in the world. Almost 1.5 million people in India work for the railway network. It has thousands of miles of track and about 23 million people use it each day.

Climate and Weather

India is known for its hot to tropical climate, but in fact it has six major climate subregions, from desert to rain forest to alpine tundra. It also has six seasons—historically named and following the ancient Hindu calendar. These are spring, summer, monsoon, autumn, pre-winter, and winter. Monsoon is a rainy season usually around July and August which is affected by winds called monsoons. They blow in from the Indian Ocean, bringing heavy rains, but they can also bring dry weather. India has three general climate periods throughout the year. It has hot and wet weather from mid-June to the end of September. There is cool and dry weather from October to February. Hot and dry weather lasts from March to mid-June.

The monsoon season in India regularly causes heavy rainfall and flooding. The amount of rainfall in some areas can be as high as 245 inches (6,220 mm). That is more than the Amazon rain forest typically gets in a year! Monsoon rains can cause problems for agriculture. Too much rain can flood fields. The retreating monsoon wind brings cool, dry air masses to parts of the country.

Monsoon flooding in the state of Kerala

Rickshaws and autorickshaws navigate monsoon floodwaters in the city of Varanasi.

About two-thirds of India's crop fields rely on rainfall for water. India has faced over 30 major **droughts** between 1871 and 2018.

Monsoons can cause flooding. The steamy weather is also often uncomfortable. Good monsoons mean water underground, rivers and lakes are replenished, and agricultural crops thrive.

Closer Look

Feeling Hot, Hot, Hot

Heat waves in India can be deadly. A heat wave is a period of extremely high temperatures that are not normal for the area. In India they typically happen from March to June and can last for weeks. One in May 2015 caused more than 2,500 deaths. A heat wave in March 2022 was the hottest in India since records began. It was also very dry. It caused around 90 deaths and a 10 to 35 percent reduction in crop yields.

Cyclones

Before or after the monsoon season, India can experience fierce tropical cyclones. Cyclones are strong spiraling storms similar to hurricanes. Winds can blow more than 100 miles (160 km) per hour. Cyclones cause very heavy rain and storm tides. About two or three cyclones make landfall in India each year.

Temperatures in most of India are warm—especially in the summer. Mountainous areas can be cold from fall through winter to spring. Along the coast, temperatures do not vary much because oceans help **moderate** temperatures. The average temperature in the interior is 81 °Fahrenheit (27 °C). Here, temperatures **fluctuate** more, going down to 56 °Fahrenheit (13 °C) in winter and up to 92 °Fahrenheit (33 °C) in summer.

Clearing up cyclone damage in West Bengal

CHAPTER 2 Becoming India

Ancient India was a melting pot of cultures and belief systems. The first humans lived there from 73,000 to 55,000 years ago. Over time, farming and city settlements developed. The northwest corner of the Indian subcontinent was known as the Indus Valley, which today spans northwestern India, great parts of Pakistan, and northeastern Afghanistan. The Indus Valley, from which India's name comes from, was home to one of the earliest known **urban** cultures in South Asia, around 2500–1700 B.C.E. This **civilization** was made up of two large cities called Harappa and Mohenjo-daro, as well as more than 100 towns and villages along the Indus River.

The Indus Valley civilization developed as people living in the mountains left their villages and moved to the valley. There was fertile soil to grow wheat, peas, sesame seeds, dates, and cotton. Natural resources made the area wealthy. Between 1900–1500 B.C.E., the cities began to be abandoned. Scientists have several theories about this, such as changes in weather patterns resulting in rivers drying up, or floods. Another theory is that trade with other countries suffered as their trading partners dealt with war in their lands.

Indus Valley people built cities known for their sophisticated planning and sewage systems that never before existed. People mined metals such as copper, which they combined with other metals to make bronze.

The people of the Indus Valley created beautiful works of art out of metals. This bronze sculpture, known as *Dancing Girl,* is from Mohenjo-daro.

Clay from the earth was turned into ceramics, and seashells from the coast were used to make pendants, rings, and beads.

Varanasi, on the banks of the Ganges River in Uttar Pradesh state, is one of the world's oldest continually inhabited cities, with artifacts dating back to 1800 B.C.E. Today it is considered a holy city that, according to lore, was established by the Hindu god Shiva.

During the Vedic period (1500–500 B.C.E.), the Vedas were written down in Sanskrit. These are the oldest hymns and **scriptures** of Hinduism. Hinduism would, over time, become India's, and the world's, third-largest religion. It has many gods, **philosophies**, and practices.

Migrations

After the collapse of the Indus Valley civilization, there were large **migrations** of other people into India. Persians migrated from their home in Iran. They settled and intermarried with Indigenous people. Groups from Southeast Asia, mainly China, and from Central Asian countries, including what we today call Kazakhstan, Turkmenistan, and Uzbekistan, also came. These migrants brought their languages, culture, traditions, religions, and knowledge. They began raising livestock. They also introduced the farming of rice. India's climate is perfect for growing rice and it soon replaced wheat as a main crop.

Crossroads of Civilizations

Over time, India became a crossroads of civilizations where people migrated to live or to trade. Each group brought their culture and belief system, which were added to the whole. There were dozens of kingdoms and **dynasties** that grew throughout ancient India. Some became great **empires** that ruled for many centuries. Beginning with the Mauryan Empire (322–185 B.C.E.) and ending with the Mughal or Timurid Empire (1526–1857 C.E.), these empires covered large territories. They built cities and governments, as well as great trade wealth and monuments to their rule. Each also had geographic centers from which they spread out and conquered more territory.

The Mauryan Empire began in the Indo-Gangetic Plain, with its capital at Pataliputra (Patna). It grew wealthy through trade with other Asian empires in China and Persia. Primarily a Hindu empire, over time, it also embraced the concepts of **Buddhism**. Many distinct kingdoms came before and several empires followed. The Mughal Empire was the last Indian empire. It was an **Islamic** empire famous for its art and architecture, and stretched through great parts of India from north to south.

Wealth and Colonialism

India's wealth, territory, and trade opportunities sparked the interest of European empires hungry to expand their own wealth and territory. By the 1600s, many Europeans were trying to secure trading routes and trading partners in Asia. The English wanted to expand their trade in India, which was known for its spices. In 1600, Queen Elizabeth I of England, later Britain, approved the founding of a trading company called the East India Company.

At first, the East India Company's merchants were welcomed by the rulers of the Mughal Empire in India. Both sides knew that trade would benefit them. The East India Company bought some land in southern India and built a fort. This soon expanded to many more forts and ports across India. Trade also expanded to include cotton, silk, **indigo**, tea, and saltpeter, a chemical used in fertilizer and fireworks.

The East India Company had its own army that battled all opposition to its control—including small kingdoms. It became a **monopoly** that wielded great power and whose iron-fisted rule caused resentments. In 1857, Indians within its own army **mutinied**, leading to a major rebellion with sieges of cities as well as an attempt to restore the Mughal Empire. In 1858, the English monarch, by this time the British Crown, stepped in to take direct control and establish British rule of India through the "India Office." This is known as the British Raj.

The Mughal emperor Humayun's tomb in Delhi was built in 1570. As the first garden tomb on the subcontinent, it inspired later Mughal architecture, such as the famous Taj Mahal. It is now a **UNESCO World Heritage Site**.

The Taj Mahal is in Agra, India, and is one of the most famous buildings in the world. It is an example of Indian architecture. It is a white marble mausoleum built by emperor Shah Jahan in memory of his wife, Mumtaz Mahal.

Mohandas "Mahatma" Gandhi was a lawyer and Indian nationalist in colonial India who used nonviolent resistance to campaign for India's independence. In 1930, he led the Salt March to resist taxes on salt and the British salt monopoly. It was a symbolic act against unjust colonial practices.

Raj Rule

The British Raj was an all-encompassing system of **colonial** rule that extended over almost all of India, and what would later become Pakistan and Bangladesh. Under the Raj, new roads, railways, and canals were built—using Indian compulsory, or forced, labor. The British also introduced new industries such as cotton and jute mills—with the profit going into British pockets. Indians resisted colonial rule and the laws enforcing it just as they had earlier fought the control of the East India Company. They did this through small acts of defiance and through larger acts of rebellion and revolt. These were met with violence by colonial forces. One form of resistance came through nonviolent civil disobedience such as strikes. Resistance also came through Indian **nationalism**, and the formation of political parties whose goal was **self-rule**.

East India Company officials enjoyed the power they had. In this East India Company painting, a company official is depicted looking like an emperor smoking a hookah and surrounded by Indian servants.

Independence and Partition

The Indian independence movement was roughly 90 years of struggle against rule by a foreign power (1857–1947). The Raj controlled almost all of India and the countries now known as Pakistan and Bangladesh. Over time, the consistent and organized opposition to British rule made it difficult for the Raj to continue. Jails were full of Indian freedom fighters, riots broke out, and Indian nationalism gained more support inside and outside the country. It was clear British rule could no longer continue. A plan was made for Britain to exit India. At midnight on August 15, 1947, India gained its independence from Britain.

The enormous territory was partitioned, or broken into two separate states: India and Pakistan. Partition was based on majority religion. India became a Hindu-majority country and Pakistan a Muslim-majority country. Partition caused a frantic, large-scale migration of 12 million people. Conflict and violence ensued. Families were separated and an estimated 2 million people were killed in acts of violence.

The Jallianwala Bagh massacre in April 1919 was a mass killing of an estimated 400 to 1,500 nonviolent protesters of colonial rule.

Painful Legacy

The brutality of the Raj and Partition left lasting scars. Many communities that co-existed along religious lines ceased to exist after Partition. Violence between Hindus and **Sikhs** and Muslims created a deep divide. The migrations continued through 1948. Today, the relationship between India and Pakistan is still tense—as are relations between Hindus and Muslims in both countries, although more Muslims live in India than in Pakistan. The India-Pakistan border is one of the most highly guarded in the world and conflict still arises, particularly over the northern mountainous region of Kashmir. There have been several wars and terrorist attacks since 1947. Both India and Pakistan also have nuclear weapons.

Soldiers guard the India-Pakistan border in Wagah in Punjab, India.

Protesters oppose a controversial change to India's Citizenship Act which grants Indian citizenship to non-Muslim religious minority groups from Pakistan, Bangladesh, or Afghanistan already living in India. Critics say religion should not be a condition of citizenship.

Jawaharlal Nehru (1889–1964) was a lawyer, author, and nationalist who was a key leader in the fight for independence. He later became first prime minister of independent India. He is shown here signing the country's **Constitution**. Nehru served from 1947 until his death in 1964. November 14, his birthday, is celebrated as Children's Day in India.

Hari Singh was the last Maharaja to rule the princely state of Jammu and Kashmir. He was a Sikh who ruled over largely Muslim subjects. Singh elected to accede to India instead of Pakistan. The territory is disputed. India controls about half of the historic area, while Pakistan controls one-third.

Building India

India launched a modernization campaign after Partition. British India had 17 provinces and 565 princely states. Princely states were states not directly ruled by the Raj, but by hereditary rulers called Rajas, Maharajas, Ranas, or Nawabs. At independence, most acceded, or handed control over, to the new countries of India or Pakistan. Together, princely states held 40 percent of the land of pre-independence India. These were integrated into the new country of India. Over time, all of India's land was organized politically and geographically into 28 states and eight union territories. India also worked on developing and modernizing its industry, farming, and infrastructure such as dams, hydropower stations, roads, and irrigation canals.

A woman is examined by a doctor in a rural health clinic in Adapur, one of the poorest states in the country.

The Indus River and its tributaries are a major water and power source for both India and Pakistan. A 1960 treaty gives India 20 percent of the water carried by the Indus system.

The construction industry employs about 50 million people in India.

Skilled workers at a LED lighting factory work at a conveyor belt.

India's growth has lifted some people out of poverty, but there is still a large wealth gap.

Industry and Economy

Before the British arrived in India, India was responsible for a quarter of the world's industrial products. Exports were products from livestock and the fertile soil, such as woolen cloth, cotton, silk, and spices. During the British Raj, trade and policies meant India's handmade product industry began to decrease. Machine-made items were brought into the country instead. At independence, industry was underdeveloped. Many of the goods that people used were imported.

It took time to modernize and develop the country's mining, steel, chemical, and shipbuilding industries—and to nurture and develop new industries. By the 1990s, India's industry had grown along with its population. Today, it is the world's fifth-largest economy. Its top industries include pharmaceuticals, software and related services, chemicals, automobiles and components, food and beverages, textiles, construction, financial services, and real estate. It also has the world's third-highest number of billionaires, at 169. Many of these people made their money in industries that didn't even exist in 1947. India's rapidly developing economy pushed 50 percent of the population into the country's **middle class** between 1990 and 2005. It continues to grow, along with the population—300 million at Partition and 1.4 billion now. It surpassed China in population growth in 2023, becoming the world's most populous country.

While the Indian economy is one of the fastest growing, it is also one of the most unequal countries. There is a large gap between the wealthy and the poor. Most ordinary Indians cannot afford health care. About 63 million more Indians are forced into poverty each year because of health care costs.

CHAPTER 3 Life Today

India is a land of many cultures, languages, beliefs, and customs. It is also a land of contrasts. Contemporary apartment buildings sit near ancient temples. Farmers use oxen to plow the land—as well as the most modern farm equipment. In some bustling cities, wealthy neighborhoods border on the crumbling housing of the poor. Traditions and festivals that date back thousands of years are made more vibrant and vital through contemporary takes on music and dance.

The Hindu festival of Holi celebrates spring, color, and love. Crowds gather at temples to sing, dance, and throw colored dye on each other.

Modern high-rises are built next to an old *dhobi ghat* where laundry is cleaned and set out to dry in Mumbai. Mumbai is the capital of Maharashtra state on the western coast of India. It is a financial and entertainment center.

Language and Belief Systems

More than 122 major languages are spoken in India. Hundreds more are spoken by smaller groups—with an estimated 1,652 "mother tongues." There is no "one" national language, but Hindi and English are official languages. Most Indians speak several languages, with Hindi, Bengali, Marathi, and Telugu being the top four first languages. Hindi is also the fourth most commonly spoken language in the world.

India is a cradle to several of the world's main religions. It is officially a **secular state** where 79 percent of the population follows Hinduism. This is an ancient belief system. Among many other practices, its followers, Hindus, believe in reincarnation, or a continuous cycle of life and death. About 14 percent of Indians are Muslim and follow the religion of Islam. Other significant religions in India include Christianity, Sikhism, **Jainism**, and Buddhism. There are also large communities of people who follow other religions. India has 705 different recognized ethnic Indigenous groups. They make up over 8 percent of India's population, or about 104 million people.

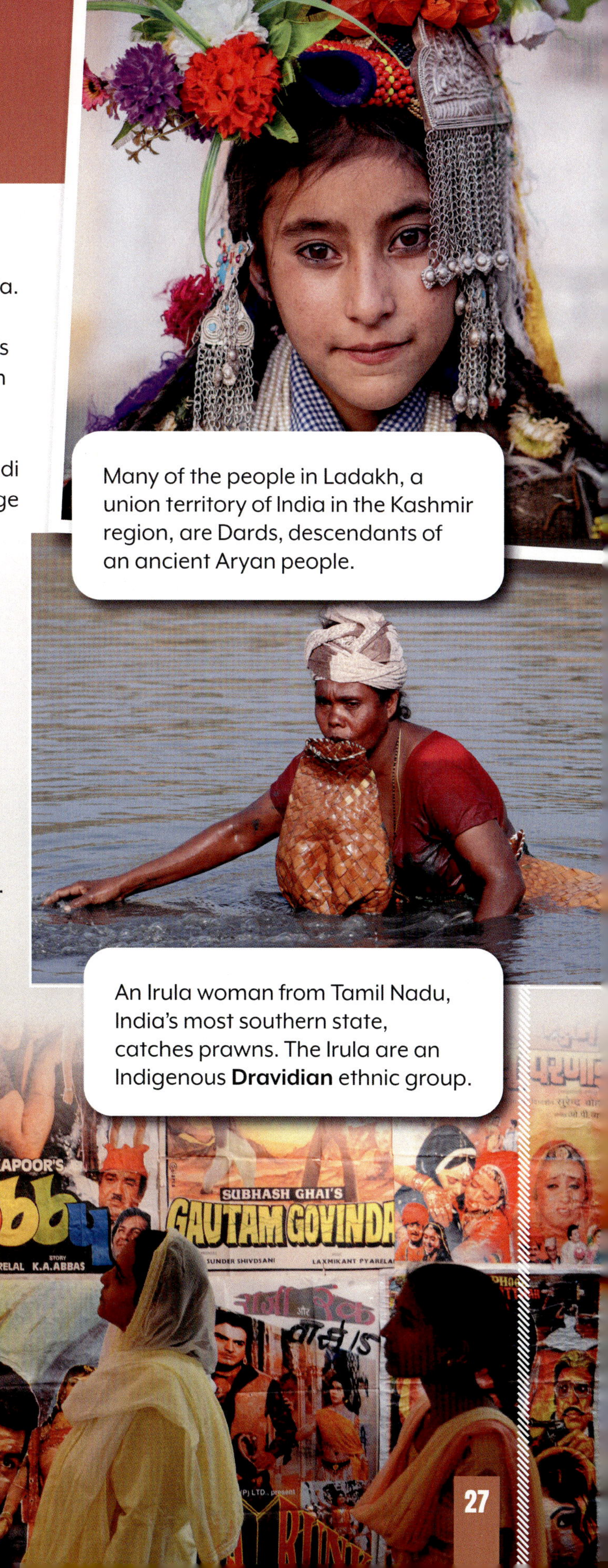

Many of the people in Ladakh, a union territory of India in the Kashmir region, are Dards, descendants of an ancient Aryan people.

An Irula woman from Tamil Nadu, India's most southern state, catches prawns. The Irula are an Indigenous **Dravidian** ethnic group.

Hindi is the most commonly used language in Indian "Bollywood" films. Here, visitors take in an exhibition of vintage Bollywood posters.

Family and Culture

One strong bond that crosses all cultures and beliefs in India is the importance of family. Traditionally, several generations of Indian families lived together in one home. Joint families are still common, although many young people now prefer to live apart, in their own homes. Parents sometimes move from one son's home to another in their old age. This allows them to care for grandchildren and to be cared for by other members of the family as they get older. Children often have strong relationships with their aunts, uncles, and cousins. Even when family does not live close by, the bonds are strong, with families keeping in close contact with those who live in other cities or countries.

Celebrations

Long weekends are common in India. There may be only three national holidays—Republic Day, Independence Day, and Gandhi Jayanti—but there are also dozens of other religious or cultural holidays that people of different religions and backgrounds celebrate. And people love to celebrate their culture. Some Hindu religious festivals last five or six days and include ceremonial rituals, get-togethers of family and friends, and always specially prepared foods. Many of these festivals have become cultural celebrations marked by everyone. Buddhists, Sikhs, and Jains for instance, also celebrate Diwali, the festival of lights that symbolizes the victory of light over darkness.

Joint family households mean grandparents help raise grandchildren, and most meals are cooked and eaten together.

Diwali is a family-focused holiday where candles, lanterns, and sometimes fireworks are lit.

Caste System Today

Social differences have a long history in India in the caste system. This system has existed in India for 3,000 years, and there are many different castes. Caste dictates what jobs, duties, and **privileges** each level, or caste, has. It also determines who they can marry. The lowest caste, the Dalits, were considered "untouchable" and were often discriminated against and overlooked. The Indian Constitution has outlawed untouchability, but it still exists. Dalits represent a large portion of mine workers. The next two lowest castes include farmers, traders, and laborers.

Ragpicking and garbage collecting are traditionally professions left to Dalits.

Kullu Dussehra is one of the biggest Hindu religious festivals in the mountainous northern state of Himachal Pradesh. It celebrates a tale told in an ancient epic poem of the death of a demon at the hands of Lord Rama, a major Hindu god.

Modern Economy

India's economy grew more slowly than its population after independence. The government favored state ownership of industry. A more open economy since the 1990s has led to growth in new industries. This has lifted more people out of poverty. Today, India is the fastest-growing economy in the world and may soon become the world's third-largest economy. This will boost manufacturing and how people live in India. Still, while the number of billionaires in the country has increased, the gap between the ultra-wealthy and the poor has also increased. The wealthiest 1 percent own more than 40 percent of India's wealth. Wealth inequality is complicated by the fact that just 18 percent of women are in the formal workforce—one of the lowest in the world. India's growth has not led to a major reduction of poverty and inequality.

Industries New and Old

One area of economic growth for India is in business **outsourcing**. This means people in India employed in jobs outside the country. Some of this is in call centers and customer service, but also software development. Industries such as energy and mining are expanding and changing. Both are important parts of India's economy. The mining industry produces over 85 minerals, and is one of the top producers of metals and minerals such as iron ore, sheet mica, zinc, manganese, and chromium. The demand for many minerals, especially those used in new technology, means India is in a position to have its mining industry contribute even more to its economy.

A warehouse in Gurugram, in the northern state of Haryana. The warehouse industry in India has grown significantly in recent years, due in part to an increase in online shopping.

Coal is India's biggest mining sector. Although India has promised to increase renewable energy to help control climate change, it is planning to reopen 100 coal mines and expand many other operating mines. More than half of India's power generation is coal-fired.

India has upgraded its infrastructure in recent years, spending a lot of money on roads, bridges, and city transportation. This is an investment in the future economy as well.

Farming Today

Agriculture is the largest livelihood provider in India. Seventy percent of rural households still depend on agriculture to support their families. Most of these are small holdings that make it hard for the farmer to make a profit. One crop failure could be serious for a farmer who is growing only one or two crops.

Agriculture in India has gone through several periods of big changes called "revolutions." The green revolution that began in the 1960s improved farm yields through machinery, **pesticides,** and fertilizers. Grain production increased as disease-resistant seeds and better irrigation methods were used. The white revolution in the 1970s focused on the dairy industry. It turned India into the world's largest milk producer. Farmers increased the size of their herds and invested in new milking sheds and equipment. Other revolutions followed, including the blue revolution in 2014, which targeted the fisheries industry. The goal was to increase fish production and fish farming. This was to ensure food, jobs, and income for its citizens.

Mangoes are the fourth-largest agricultural crop in India. Known as the "King of Fruits," mangoes grow in the hills and valleys of Himachal Pradesh, the northernmost state in India.

Workers collect raw cotton by hand for the ginning process at a factory in Madhya Pradesh state in central India. India is the world's largest producer of cotton and jute and second-largest producer of silk. The textile industry employs over 35 million people, many of them semi-skilled workers.

Tea pickers harvest leaves by hand in Assam, the country's largest tea-producing state. After China, India is the largest producer of tea in the world. There are 10 major tea-producing states in the country.

CHAPTER 4

A Vibrant Culture

Indian people often formally greet others by clasping their hands together and saying hello, welcome, or how are you in their own languages.

"*Namaste*," "*Salaam*," "*Kem cho*," "*Nomoshkar*," "*Vanakkam*"...in a land of hundreds of languages and many cultures, strangers and loved ones are greeted with different languages and customs. India's ancient past is the source of many traditions, as well as ideas and inventions.

One of the oldest civilizations in the world, India is the birthplace of yoga. Yoga is an ancient practice that combines poses, concentration, and deep breathing to develop mental peace. It was first mentioned in the Hindu *Rigveda*, the oldest Sanskrit book, dating back 1500 to 1000 B.C.E. Today, yoga is practiced throughout the world.

India is also known for its classical music and dance. Indian classical music evolved over time into different northern and southern Indian styles. Both are unlike European classical music in melody and timing. They also use instruments that originated in South Asia. These include stringed instruments that are plucked, such as the sitar and rudra veena, and hand drums such as the tabla, mridangam, and others. Indian classical dance also has ancient roots and is often performed today at festivals.

A watercolor painting from 1735 showing a Rajasthani woman playing a tanpura, a stringed instrument played in classical Indian music.

A small group of classical musicians play Karnatak music at a Hindu temple.

Bhangra is a folk dance from the Sikh community in Punjab, a state in northern India that borders on Pakistan. It was traditionally performed at harvest festivals. Today there are Bhangra dance contests. It is often danced to Bhangra music, a form of folk-pop music which features South Asian and European instruments.

Music and Bollywood

Many Indian musicians today combine Indian classical instruments and traditions with popular music styles and genres such as folk, rap, rock, dub, and pop. One form of Indian popular music heard around the world is Hindu film or Bollywood music. Bollywood is India's film industry and almost all of the roughly 2,000 films made each year are musicals—many with elaborate dance scenes. It is a major, multi-billion dollar industry and its stars, like Hollywood actors, are known around the world. Most Bollywood films are produced in the Hindi language, but there are also many Tamil and Telugu language films. Bollywood is centered in Mumbai, formerly known as Bombay.

Priyanka Chopra is a Bollywood and Hollywood actress and former winner of the Miss World 2000 pageant. She has been ranked as one of the world's 100 most powerful women.

A classical dancer performs a South Indian Tamil-style dance.

Many Beliefs

India is a spiritual country, where religious customs and beliefs have long influenced the way people live. It is the birthplace of Hinduism, or Sanatana Dharma, an ancient religion and way of life that has the third-largest following in the world. More than 1 billion Hindus live in India. Sanatana Dharma has many beliefs, rituals, and practices. There are more than 2 million Hindu temples in India, many with shrines to the countless Hindu gods. The country is also home to about 173 million Muslims, who believe in one god, Allah. Buddhism is another major ancient religion that arose in South Asia. Siddhartha Gautama, the Buddha, wandered the lands of ancient India seeking enlightenment and died in northern India. Today there are 8.4 million Buddhists in India. Christianity came to India in 52 C.E. Today there are about 26 million Christians in India—making it the third-largest religion in the country.

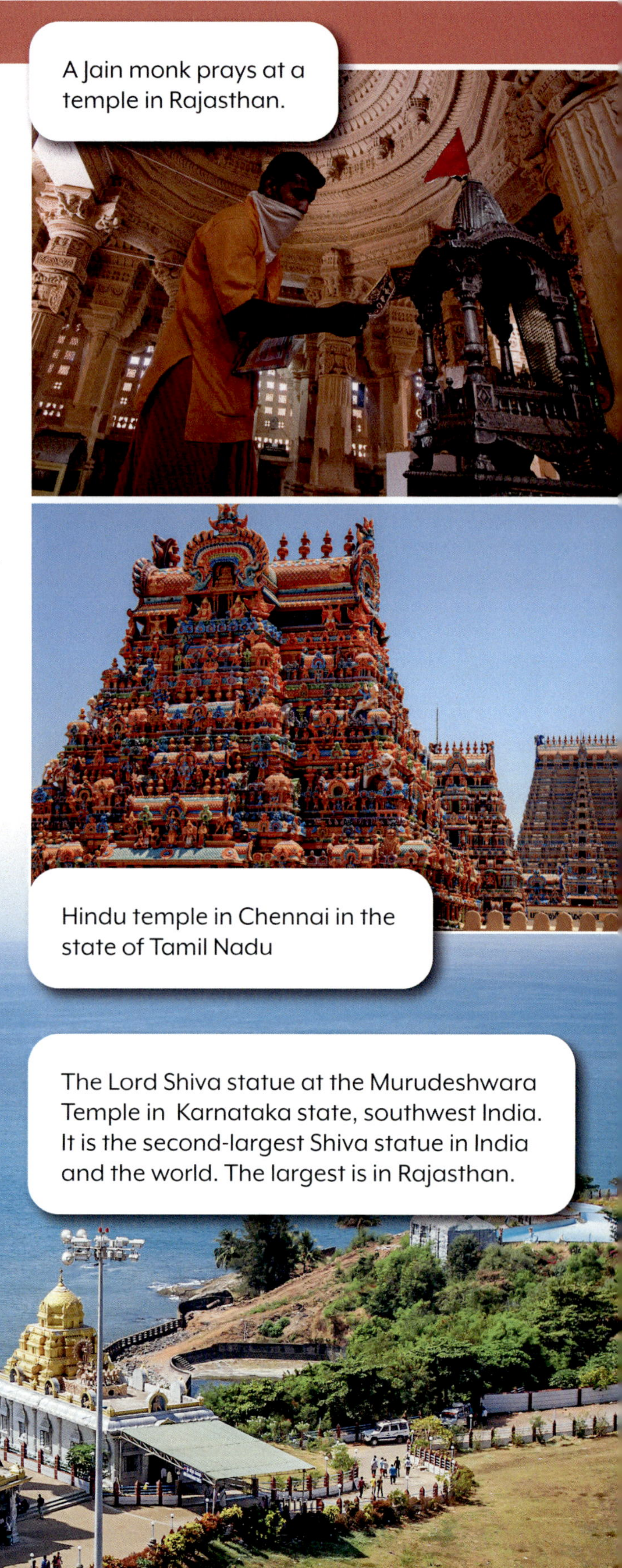

A Jain monk prays at a temple in Rajasthan.

Hindu temple in Chennai in the state of Tamil Nadu

The Lord Shiva statue at the Murudeshwara Temple in Karnataka state, southwest India. It is the second-largest Shiva statue in India and the world. The largest is in Rajasthan.

Muslims pray outside of Delhi's Jama Masjid.

Sikhism is a faith founded on the Indian subcontinent in the mid-1400s. About 21 million Sikhs live in India. The Golden Temple of Amritsar, in Punjab, is one of Sikhism's holiest sites. Jainism is one of the oldest religions in India and the world, with its roots in the Indus Valley civilization. There are about 4.4 million Jains in India. Judaism has a more than 2,800-year history in India. Many kept their religious traditions but adopted local Indian cultures. The Jewish community today is small—an estimated 5,000 people. There are also many "folk" religions in India. Some are people who follow the remnants of ancient belief systems.

India is the largest democracy in the world and officially a secular state according to its Constitution. People are free to follow whatever beliefs they want to. However, there has been increasing harassment and violence against and between religious groups.

Indian Christians pray at a church in Kerala.

The Golden Temple, or Harmandir Sahib, was completed in 1604. It features gold encrusted interior walls and a gold chandelier.

CHAPTER 4

Cultures and Traditions

Indian culture reflects a strong respect for elders, families, and hard work. Religious values are infused in the overall culture. Hindus consider cattle sacred. They believe cattle are a symbol of life and should be protected. Cattle roam the streets as they wish and traffic and people move around them. Hindus do not eat beef or kill cattle—although milk-based foods are a part of their diet and many traditional Indian foods. Krishna, one of the major Hindu gods, was a cowherd who was known to be fond of ghee, or clarified butter. Ghee is used in cooking, as well as Hindu religious ceremonies and even traditional medicine.

India is also the largest producer and consumer of milk in the world. Many Indian foods are made with milk or other dairy products, including *lassi*, a smoothie-like drink made from yogurt, *kulfi*, or Indian ice cream, *kheer*, a milky pudding made from rice or other grains, and *gulab jamun*, a sweet doughball made with milk and cheese.

Cricket was introduced to India in the 1700s, but really took off in the 1900s. There have even been Bollywood movies based on cricket, including the 2001 film *Lagaan*, about a village new to cricket that beats a British army team during the Raj.

Cattle roam freely in a market in Varanasi.

Firecrackers and sparklers are popular during Diwali celebrations.

Gulab jamun is a sweet dessert made mainly from milk solids. It is often eaten at festivals and other celebrations.

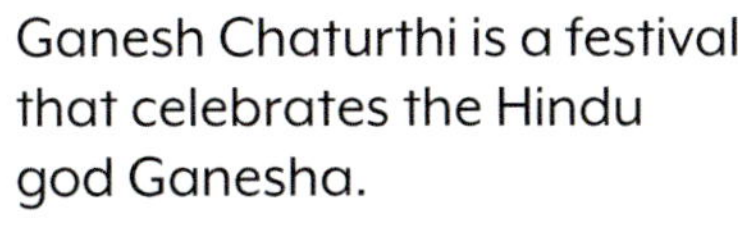

Ganesh Chaturthi is a festival that celebrates the Hindu god Ganesha.

A kulfi vendor sells from his cart in Delhi.

Celebration Time

Food, music, and often dance are a big part of Indian celebrations—no matter their religious roots. Diwali, or the Festival of Lights, is the biggest and most important festival in India. It is a Hindu festival that many Indians of other religions also mark. Diwali celebrates the triumph of light over darkness, and good over evil. Lamps are lit in streets and homes, and fireworks are set off. Celebrations are also a time to dress up and gather with family and friends to eat. Some celebrations happen spontaneously, such as when a favorite team wins a cricket match!

Cricket is a national passion. It is the most popular sport and is played all over the country—in leagues of men, women, and children. People even play it in the street. The Indian Premier League, a men's cricket league that has 10 teams, is the most popular cricket league in the world. The India men's national cricket team, nicknamed the Men in Blue, has won the Cricket World Cup twice, in 1983 and 2011.

Dressed for the Occasion

Dressing for the occasion is an important part of celebrations and events in India, and Indians, no matter where they live, are not afraid to dress colorfully. Traditional Indian clothing is versatile, bold, and made with a variety of fabrics to suit climates and purposes. Traditional clothing is also influenced by local or regional cultures and religions. Although something may be labeled as traditional, it is often still worn as everyday clothing. In India, even casual "Western" clothing often has a South Asian "twist."

Traditional clothing is often made from vibrant silk or cotton fabrics.

Saris are a traditional women's garment made from a long strip of cloth, draped in over 100 different ways. Women in some regions also wear long skirts called *lehenga choli*. Traditionally, some Indian men wear dhotis. These are long unstitched garments tied at the waist and ankles. They are often worn with a kurta, a loose, collarless tunic. Muslim women and men often wear *salwar kameez*, or long tunics with pajama-style trousers. In fact, the word pajama and the pants themselves are Indian in origin, as are nose rings, and the riding pants called jodhpurs.

Traditional clothing varies throughout the country according to culture and climate. Men sometimes wear dhotis and kurtas, while women often wear saris.

Indian Weddings

Weddings are special events that unite and join families. They vary according to religion, but always feature vibrant clothing, music, and lots of food. Traditionally, Indian marriages were arranged by parents of the bride and groom. Today, more marriages are "love matches." Many Hindu, Jain, and Sikh marriages include several steps and traditions. If a family can afford it, weddings are enormous—with 300 to 1,000 guests, and a lot of food and dancing. Wedding celebrations happen over a number of days, and often include a mehndi party, where the bride has her hands and feet decorated with ornamental patterns made from mendhi dye. Traditionally, brides wear red saris or lehenga, and grooms wear sherwani suits and dhotis or *veshtis*—long cloths around their waists.

Weddings include the gift of many pieces of head-to-toe jewelry for the bride—as expensive and ornate as a family can afford. Each piece has significance. The jewelry becomes part of the bride's wealth.

CHAPTER 5

Looking to the Future

Like many countries that have emerged from colonialism to carve a future, India has faced many challenges. The future will present more. The environment is one **priority** for keeping the population, natural world, and industry healthy. Pollution and climate change are two big issues India is attempting to address. An estimated 90 percent of the country is already affected by heat waves that are further fueled by climate change. Heat waves already hit temperatures of more than 120 °Fahrenheit (49 °C). India has committed to the the United Nation's **Sustainable** Development Goals, which include measures to reduce the impact of heat waves, such as planting more trees. Trees and cooling areas in cities can help lower temperatures and offer people a place to rest in shade. India also has a plan to create "green railways" with net-zero carbon emissions by 2030. Net-zero emissions means that it will balance the amount of greenhouse gases it releases into the atmosphere with the amount it takes out.

Protecting glaciers, reducing single-use plastic, and producing clean cooking fuel are other global warming protection measures India is targeting.

India is fourth on the list of countries most affected by climate change. Severe weather is impacting all parts of the country.

India's coal power generation is one of the causes of climate change. Burning coal gives off greenhouse gases such as carbon dioxide which trap heat close to Earth's surface. India has plans to move to more non-fossil fuel energy by 2030. This would also help with air pollution.

Water Scarcity

Both wells and river systems are vital sources of water for the hundreds of millions of people who use them to bathe, drink, and irrigate their crops. Untreated sewage is polluting surface and groundwater. More than 100 Indian cities dump untreated sewage into the Ganges alone. Pesticides and fertilizers from agricultural runoff on farms also find their way into water systems. The problem is there are not enough water treatment plants for the size of the population, or they are closed due to maintenance, staffing, or electricity problems. By 2021, India's government had built enough treatment plants to treat 50 percent of wastewater. It is estimated that another 4,500 treatment plants would need to be built for 100 percent treatment of wastewater.

The Indian government is planning to upgrade the national rail system. This includes all-electric railways, upgrading and expanding existing rail lines, and building a high-speed train network across the country.

A new wastewater treatment facility in Delhi

Future of Industries

The technology industry is India's future. The tech sector is booming with new businesses starting up and established businesses expanding. This industry includes more than 17,000 companies and employs over 5 million people. India has a lower cost of living and cheaper labor than many countries in Europe and North America. This means companies outsource a lot of services to India. The Indian government is encouraging growth in the outsourcing sector by establishing Software Technology Parks of India (STPI). This organization helps companies get started, create new products, and make more connections overseas.

India has also created Special Economic Zones (SEZ). These are areas in which business and trade laws are different from the rest of the country. Laws in SEZs make it easier for businesses to develop, hire people, and trade with other nations. Manufacturing in India is moving to using machines with intelligent automation. This means combining artificial intelligence (AI) with robots. This helps companies work more efficiently and cut costs.

Software "tech parks" are designed for the tech industry. There are several "hubs" throughout the country.

Feeding India

Agriculture in India needs to change to feed a growing population. Biotechnology is the science of working with the cells of plants to make new products. India wants to use biotechnology to develop crops that resist disease, are hardier in the face of climate change, and are more nutritious. Sensors and drones will help regulate and manage fertilizing, watering, and harvesting.

These peppers are being grown with plastic "mulching" film. The film acts as a heat and cold insulator. Mulching helps prevent soil erosion as well.

Two agricultural scientists discuss crop growth at a test farm. Today, India has one of the world's largest agricultural research systems.

Future changes

In overtaking China as the most populous country in the world, India inherits a title that carries a lot of challenges. These include feeding, housing, and employing all of its citizens, as well as keeping them healthy.

Education will be a major factor for India moving forward. The culture that gave the world the **Fibonacci numbers** in 200 B.C.E. will need to continue innovating. The tech sector needs a new generation with the skills for a changing employment landscape. This includes preparing the workforce to move from traditional small-scale agriculture to technology. The participation of women in the workforce means education will need to keep pace. It is something that India can do. At the time of Partition in 1947, the literacy rate was 18 percent. Three-quarters of a century later, it is 77 percent—a testament to improved education.

Future doctors train at a medical college in Lucknow, Uttar Pradesh state.

Workers build new roads in rural areas of Maharashtra.

The Delhi Metro opened in 2002.

Commuters wait for taxis and buses near Howrah Bridge in Kolkata.

Regional Differences

India is trying to address regional differences in opportunities in education and jobs. This will again increase the country's middle class. Good education, access to the digital world, and health care are lacking in some regions today. A lack of good roads affects India's ability to grow its economy. Although it has tripled its highways in the last 20 years, they are not all of good quality. Only 3 percent are national highways and most only have two lanes. Forty percent of the roads are dirt roads and a third of Indian villages do not have all-weather roads. Highways are **congested** and not well maintained. The difficulties are lack of money and problems with the states and federal government working together to plan and manage the projects.

A healthy and sustainable future is vital as India's population grows. Affordable health care and access to care in rural areas are two main issues. Unhealthy food and lifestyles shorten life spans in both urban and rural areas. Healthier lives depend on India dealing with air and water pollution. Nine out of 10 of the world's most air-polluted cities are in India, including the capital, New Delhi. Tackling these problems will allow India to unlock its potential to create a healthy and sustainable future.

administer To control or govern

agrarian society A community whose economy is based on farmland, raising animals, and producing crops

arid Having very little rain or water

Buddhism A religion that originated in ancient India and spread to China and throughout Southeast Asia

civilization An advanced stage of human culture and development

climate change The long-term changes of the world's temperature and weather patterns

collide To hit forcefully while moving

colonial Relating to a colony, or a country or area occupied by and under the control of another country

congested Crowded with people or vehicles

Constitution The basic laws and principles by which a country is governed

cultivate To grow crops

desertification The process of how land becomes desert, such as through drought or deforestation

Dravidian A family of languages, including Tamil and Telugu, spoken mostly in southern India. Also, the people and culture of southern India and Sri Lanka.

droughts Long periods of no rain

dynasty A family of rulers in which power is passed down

empires Groups of countries and colonies under a single authority

exported Sold goods or services to another country

Fibonacci numbers A series or sequence of numbers important to mathematics which were first described in ancient Indian Sanskrit writings

fluctuate To continually change back and forth

foreign national A person who is living in or visiting a country where they are not a citizen

glacier A mass of ice formed mostly over the last ice age, located mainly on mountains or at Earth's poles

Hindu A person who follows the religion of Hinduism, based on a belief system originating in ancient India

Indigenous Native to a particular place. Indigenous people are the original inhabitants of a place.

indigo A blue dye made from a plant

Islamic Related to the worldwide religion of Islam, a faith revealed by Allah through the prophet Muhammad. Followers of Islam are called Muslims.

Jainism A religion with roots in ancient India that teaches practicing nonviolence for all living things

labor-intensive A process or industry that requires a lot of labor to produce goods or services

mangroves Trees and shrubs that grow in salt or brackish water near coastlines in tropical areas

middle class Used to describe a group of people whose incomes and tastes are between higher and lower social ranks

migration Movement from one place to another

moderate Something that is not extreme

monopoly Complete control of a service or supply of goods

mutinied Revolted or rebelled against some authority

nationalism Devotion or patriotism to one's country

outsource To contract out jobs or services

pesticides Chemicals that destroy plant or animal pests

philosophies Methods of investigating truths, knowledge, or behavior

plateau A large area of high, flat ground

populated Inhabited by people

priority Of the highest importance

privileges Special benefits or advantages

sacred Connected to gods or religion

Sanskrit The ancient language of India, used in ancient books and scriptures

scripture Sacred writings

secular state A government that is neutral in matters of religion

sediment Plant, mineral, or other matter that settles to the bottom of a liquid

self-rule Government of a country or area by the people that live there

sickle A short-handled farming tool with a semi-circular blade used for cutting grain or grass

Sikhs The people who follow the religion of Sikhism, which originated in the Punjab region

submerged Below the surface of water

sustainable Capable of being sustained, or supported for the future

tributaries Rivers or streams flowing into larger rivers or lakes

UNESCO World Heritage site A protected landmark or area singled out by the United Nations Educational, Scientific, and Cultural Organization as being globally significant

union territories Territories which are under the control of the Republic of India

urban Densely populated areas such as cities or towns

Books

DK. *Illustrated Atlas of India: A Visual Guide to the Land, Its People and Culture*. DK Children, 2020.

Gupta, Subhadra Sen. *A Children's History of India.* Rupa Publications, 2015.

Manning, Paul. *Ganges River.* Smart Apple Media, 2015.

Websites

www.kids-world-travel-guide.com/india-for-kids.html
See the world through children's eyes with Kids World Travel Guide to India.

https://kids.nationalgeographic.com/geography/countries/article/india
Explore India with National Geographic Kids.

www.theschoolrun.com/homework-help/india
Take a quiz about India, learn to cook Indian food, and listen to Bollywood songs with The School Run.

About the Author

Natalie Hyde has written over 100 fiction and non-fiction books for young readers. Exploring new cultures, traditions, and of course, food, is something she loves to do on her travels.